Anything but the Moon

Anything but the Moon

GEORGE SIPOS

Edited by Sue Sinclair.
Cover illustration by Brand X Pictures.
Cover design by Julie Scriver.
Book design by Lisa Rousseau.
Printed in Canada.
10 9 8 7 6 5 4 3 2 1

Library and Archives Canada Cataloguing in Publication

Sipos, George, 1949-
Anything but the moon / George Sipos.

Poems.
ISBN 0-86492-427-5

I. Title.

PS8637.I65A65 2005   C811'.6   C2005-903502-1

Published with the financial support of the Canada Council for the Arts, the Government of Canada through the Book Publishing Industry Development Program, and the New Brunswick Culture and Sports Secretariat.

Goose Lane Editions
469 King Street
Fredericton, New Brunswick
CANADA E3B 1E5
www.gooselane.com

This book is for Bridget.

I begin to believe the only sin is distance, refusal.
Jane Hirshfield

Table of Contents

ONE

TWO

THREE

FOUR

ONE

Henhouse

Out in the dark beyond the trees
the chickens roost
like shoes in a closet.
Their minds, unlaced, clutch only
the needlessness
of thinking anything, of getting on.

They cluck a little, shit, refuse to dream.

In the morning you find them jostling
by the gate. Rickshaw drivers
desperate to take you anywhere, they invent
frantic itineraries in the dirt
(beak, pinfeathers, claw, whatever you want),
make you feel rich
as you scatter the small change
of an indifferent husbandry.

If there is any point to this
it is in the silent temple
where you have strewn
marigolds on the straw
and removed your sandals
before an Isa Brown brooding in her box.
She may let you slip your hand beneath her
toward the ivory warmth
of an egg, or she may peck you.

It is early.

The brown eye
of the world looks back at you
unblinking.

Dapple

Not cloud-dappled
    as in landscape
but as in sky
    as in aquarium
where clouds swim by each other
each species unto itself
its accustomed depth, its
preferred way of flicking a fin
of fanning water over gills,
a liquid wind
coming and going, the invisible
exchange of oxygen.

The clouds today have forgotten
the simple rule fish know that
relative motion is a condition of life,
that water becomes
    air becomes water
in the updrafts of air, the circling
currents of the sea.

Some have sunk
dappling earth with their bodies,
a few vanished
bleached
    by the rarity of it all —

a thin blue wash
what's left of buoyancy
        of breath.

Swing

Wells, B.C.

Summertime, and they're all at the river,
clover in the schoolyard fragrant with bees,
swings lazy as sunflowers against a wall,
a dog ambling
　　across the street.

Summertime,
and the clocks have all flown north
to roost on the tundra.
It is recess and
someone has lost the bell,
as my feet swing
in
out
arms looped lightly
around the chains —
the sweet nausea of motion
as the sky tips, as
the world
　　comes and goes.

How can I stop this flight
these houses, these clouds,
put the brakes to this spinning earth —
heel scraping in dirt
like a finger tracing
an etched sentence

chalk on slate.

The Syntax of Summer

How different the wind in summer,
the vocabulary of trees, speech
spilling from leaves in easy sibilance,
whole groves of aspen nodding assent
to whatever is said in
the prevailing consensus of air.

The stories of summer must be true —
the way the sun
rises already hot at 6:00 a.m.,
how its light is filtered green along the fenceline,
how kernels swell in seedheads,
timothy and fescue bending
to the recursive
burden
    of the nameable world.

What voice for the sceptic
in all this   airtime
for the long phonemic breath of winter,
the density
    of uninflected air
that arrives in the night from the pole,
seeps through wool,
    seeks bone.

That writes on the land in drifts.

August

At 3:00 a.m. you pee, let the cat in,
and realize you've left
the water running in the garden.
Is it worse to have forgotten,
or to know that this late in the summer
it matters little either way?

On hot afternoons years ago
you threw a ball against
the back of the house for hours at a time
till your father yelled to stop or the bricks would come loose and
the wall collapse.
It didn't of course (though
who knows whether the house
still stands) but the point was
that anything, however unlikely,
was thinkable then — the ball
going *thunk* against brick,
coming back to you.

Above the rows of yellowed pea-vines
droplets rise from the sprinkler,
lose momentum,
fall.

Year
after year
you plant a garden, then lose interest.

Night after night
the cat
scratches at the screen.
You let her in.

Soccer, Fall

rain, all day, and
you on the soggy field
running on the wing
all arms and legs
hair wet against temples
your eyes
on the play, always
elsewhere

you are sixteen
you are learning
to ignore the weather
to feel in
your thin muscles
the tug of abstraction
what it means to yearn
at a distance, learning
to move over the earth
to be always thinking
of something else,
to be ready

and I, huddled
in the notional shelter
of an umbrella
do I long for the play
to come your way
water spraying from
facets of leather as
the ball rolls toward
the brief moment
when you
become the centre of everything
when you alone
propel the world
your clean-hearted faith
in getting it right

I want to witness those
gestures of grace
your feet more intricate
than fingers
what they can do
the way your body moves
beyond grass and rain
the way you lean
into thought

but the cold, the dampness
in my bones
make me wish the ball away
afraid
not that you'll stumble
not that the girl in blue
will elbow you aside
but that you'll succeed beyond your hopes
break away down the side
legs a blur, the ball
spurting forward, and you
diminish toward
the dubious triumph
of the distant net
the goal

I want to keep you
like this
the awkward elegance
of waiting
the sound only
of your boots as you
run by, and I
in the rain with your wristwatch
keeping it dry
and ticking

Late Season

This is not how it should end —
hay mouldering unbaled,
windrows in fields subsiding
day by day —
what remains of summer
shrugging its shoulders
into fall.

It's not just the waste,
though the practical heart
may mourn even that, but
the neglect, the way hope
leaches out of things,
decay settling in till
the world remembers no reasons
but those which sink into soil.

This is not how it began —
in sunlight and wind,
a red tractor circling
a green field, a blue sky,
slender stalks of grass
lying down among crickets,
everything that could be dreamt
fragrant among all that hay.

Who can remember what came next?
Night, of course
and dawn. The sound of rain.
A pale light soaking the stubble.
It's what you get
for living in the North, where
the weather changes because
        that's what weather does.

But rain explains so little:
the blunting of light perhaps,
a certain disappointment
    (the fragrance of hay being
    fleeting in any case)
but not
an entire season's despair, not
the mass extinction of crickets,
the tractor hanging by its neck
from the rafters of the shed.

Maybe the abandoned fields
are letters of farewell,
but who is left to read them?
Line after line
    the geese fly south,
trace the contours of
an emptying world, their wings
like fingers, like scythes
mowing a swath
through what's left
uncut.

Charango

Rain today.

A young couple sits on the sidewalk by the Credit Union, their backs against a wall under an overhang. I see them when I drive off to the Post Office, and again when I return. They sit beside a large bag, so one of them is possibly leaving. The girl is blond; her companion tanned, like someone who has spent time in the bush. They are talking, telling each other stories. I watch the girl run her fingers through her hair.

Across the parking lot two musicians from the Andes shelter by the drugstore. One is playing pan-pipes, the other a charango. Their amplified music carries unnaturally across the distance. After each song the charango player speaks into his microphone. "Thank you," he says. "Thank you very much. Thank you." But he speaks to no one. Not a single person stops to listen in the rain.

Whose is the greater sadness: These musicians going through the motions of pretending a wet shopping centre is not the sum total of all there is in the world? Or the young couple, unaware that this half-hour may be the happiest they will ever know? Their words coming so easily. The touch of their shoulders so light, so uncomplicated. Their lives never again this carelessly poised.

Thirty years from now who will recall this rain? How simple everything seemed, how accidental? I know no one will remember a red truck with a white canopy, a sheaf of envelopes mailed, Robert Silverman playing Brahms on the radio — the piano concerto he wrote in Tuscany where he had gone to escape the incessant damp of a Viennese spring.

When the piano stops there is only silence. The engine turning off.

I lock the door. Leave the lovers to their thanks. Walk back to work in the rain.

Flurry

What did you expect?
That the evasions of autumn
would just go on,
seedheads of fireweed and thistle,
the drift of leaves,
geese above the hayfields
quoting Proust forever?
Who were you trying to kid?

Wind blows through branches,
slides across films of ice.
The north sides of things
have already forgotten sunlight.
Even the vegetables in the garden
have had the decency to turn brown
and lie down.

And now this snowfall
this flurry —
a skyful of vowels
through which your ear strains
for the merest memory of syntax,
a blurred background of spruce,
whatever residual green
you can hold on to
before soil turns white,
grasses bend,
and the texture of the world
fades to outline.

Stella

All winter we dream of spring:
what I'll say
what you'll reply
how it will be —
    a warm wind, water
glistening at eaves, daylight on the brink
once again, of fragrance.

We can believe anything in the dark,
rehearse the return of soil,
                of birdsong,
the aptness of speech, how lucid
bodies can become in an abundance of light,
and how much more we stand to
gain than lose when
the clocks move ahead.

But snow still falls in April.
The season will not budge.
In the half-light of dawn
the brainwaves of the furnace cycle
through the stages of sleep
while we dream
an elusive landfall.

Only the cat stays awake all night,
returns to the threshold
in the morning
white fur matted with mud,
clay between claws,
an olive branch jaunty in her teeth
                and reeking
to high heaven.

A Blue Bowl

Spring sunlight
spills through windows,
you tell me,
like liquid gold poured
from the crucible of winter.

I reply with some arcana about
the refractive index of glass,
angles of incidence, the laws
as I would have them
                  of reflection.

Thus we debate
the optics of a changing season —
you with your devotion
to the impulsive alchemy of light,
your belief in the philosopher's stone
of the heart and the eye,
                  and I
with my careful calculations
of distance and attitude,
all I have learned
about the mathematics of lengthening days.

But light, which is neither wave
nor particle,
performs its miracles
without the aid of diagrams,
and the lenses of the world
are polished
with a finer dust
than you or I might admit.

All by itself
day becomes longer than night.
Oranges glow in a blue bowl
by the window.

TWO

Hay

Such operatic summers —
heat, diesel smoke,
haying to the sound of thunder
from clouds towering in the west,
bales against knees, frayed denim, the dust
of dried clover, golden slant
of sun mingling
with sweat in our eyes,
                              the rush
to get it all in.

It is the difficult things I cling to: the way
the tines of a pitch-fork
are polished with use,
the way the muscles of neck and
shoulders strain to heave
bales into the sky.

              I want
a language made of thunder,
and the moments of air
before thunder,
of the anvil-heads
counting down
              from lightning.

I want words that cut nylon,
words sharp enough for the snap
of twine,
for the brief expansion of
dried timothy and brome,
      of the lungs,
of so much held breath released

fragrant as cut grass.

Bow Falls

Not a falls so much
as a gloss,

the water white and boisterous
its brief passage over
tilted strata
a flood of six-
teenth notes with
no rests all
headlong below banks.

You have traveled so far
to be here, this place
between upper and lower
silences, that
you wish away
the tidy viewpoints
        and guardrails,

want only water and
wind in a wild place,
a phrasing so far beyond intention
it's caught
                somewhere
between breath and breath,

a melody that simple, a fall
that accidental.

What do you call

that play of light on water that's
not exactly sparkle
nor crystal
nor tiara, or *eau petillant*
tingle, fanfare
fish scale scraped on a slab of lapis,
not a schoolyard at recess
or Bach, or Binoche by candlelight
or crickets, or meteors,
not the melting of ice, or flight
of birds, tang
of lemon
trill
spill of beads
shiver of aspen shaken by a breeze
on the eastern slope of the Rocky Mountains at the moment
a cloud's shadow slips over a white-tailed deer and
she stops   her heart
trembling in that instant because it can't help it?

Not that.
But something like it. Something
that escapes us, here by the river, where
sun and water make us forget
the simplest words:
words like *yes*
maybe
like
do you understand what I mean?

There is so little we are sure of,
and yet these currents
can convince us of anything: the sigh of
water flowing by, the
needlessness of speech,
how easily light becomes liquid, and how
our drinking has nothing
whatever
to do with thirst.

Prescribed Burn

It's just something in the air, you said,
    a haze,
light smudging the distance
as in old photographs, those soft snaps
caught somewhere between sepia and the
first shy fumblings
of Ektachrome, a fading
you mistake for desire.

Maybe so. In the age of the pixel
we believe we are past all danger
of memory, the fragrant
chromaticism of wood smoke
caught in wool, in hair,
               only a few
small captions left, words
barely legible,
the story almost lost
in a thin sloping hand.

It's no use talking about humidity
or barometric pressure, or
management studies on selective thinning of the understorey.
None of this is under control.
Somewhere in the hills the heart climbs
through brushwood,
spills flame, drips
crimson into tinder till the trees
flash like magnesium, catch

a world breathless,
overexposed,
      utterly without plan.

Yard Work

What are you trying to say
you asked,

        missing the point.

While I
in the unexpected Spring
dragged branches to the bonfire along a path
that switched from snow to soil and
back to what remained white and cupped and crusted,
the repetition of coming and going
like terms of a seasonal syllogism:
something simply demonstrable,
like the need for yard work.

But I don't think it's so easily put.

Where snow meets soil, seedlings of spruce
pierce the melting edge
and assert their green syllables
into the argument of the afternoon
with such delicate abundance
I am brought to a halt
each time.
How can I go on
with my armful of brush for the burning,
tread on the pliant needles
as if the work,
and not they, were the point?

It is not disclosure
    I want to tell you
that matters between us
(the profuse logic or illogic of so much green
against the snow)
but our moments of avoidance:
a foot caught in mid-stride
with no idea at all
   where it might land.

Arete

We have walked the windy edge:
such careful footsteps
ice axe   boots
the precautions we know;
so high up this
rib of rock
we don't dare look down,
plunging blue space everywhere
an impossible horizon.

And wind —
the air so thin,
our words
the vaguest of gestures —
not enough breath
for what we might mean.

How long can a rope be
between two people,
coils sliding between fingers
like the stories we invent as we go —
frayed
tenuous
          as if their passage
could keep us from falling?

Spray River

The trail leads nowhere but to the bridge
through open forest, pines.

We are ill-shod. Our words falter
through mud and slivers of ice.
But the valley is forgiving.
We walk barefoot over stones.

The river has so many voices
we have never heard,
and they speak at once, distinctly.

We walk on an ice-floe caught
on a sandbar.
There is no danger.

A pebble out of water is stone;
in the water still stone.
Where does sorrow come from
if not from stone?

They will ask about wildlife;
we will say no, only squirrels.
We will say yes.

I have brought two oranges, you hand cream.

The bridge arcs across the river
                a narrow gap
the other side.

Sweetwater Road

Riding east with you in the dark
what I need to know is
where the border falls,
                              whether
the lights ahead are Alberta or still
the safe side
of a landscape I have never seen —
but *maybe*
is the most you'll say, as if lines on a map
mean nothing here,
as if once through the Pine Pass
        having lost my bearings
        in that winding winter cordillera
I should be done with limits,
done with the need to fill unfilled
corners of maps — just give in

to this *terra incognita* rolling by.

But there's more to it,
more than empty fields caught in your headlights,
than snow drifting from god knows where
across the road.

If you stopped the car and you and I got out
we would find ourselves at the very edge
(however dark, however windswept)
of the world,
feet touching earth
at the one precise point of passage
between surface and aquifer,
between what we think
and what we might
        bring ourselves to say:

that
impossible intersection,
    random roadside,
place to dig.

There is no end to clean water

You never open curtains
but with grace,
the way grass moves
at the edge of a stream
(one side and the other)
your wrist loose, the
way your arm
    strokes the bow.

There is so little to weep for —
river liquid around your ankles,
    blue sky, streambed,
whatever is reflected, whatever
inside.

Here, anything you might say
is true, speech spilling so
lightly over gravel,
                  fish
a flicker
at the edge of the eye,
don't look

      for the downstroke,
thud of bird against glass,
the clench of muscle that will
hurl you into air,
the line of horizon a filament
clear as the sky,
thin as the gap in the curtain.

Circle Lake

Someone has been ice-fishing,
punctured the lake like a cancelled ticket,
left lines of tangled footprints
and is now gone
                    like the year,
over as routinely as that

It's surprising how little it takes
to render the solstice safe,
to bear the weight of this passage
                    from loss
to whatever is
its possible alternative —
lines we dangle
into the impossibly pale
blue of the mid-winter sky

the departure of light
confused
by a few pink clouds, as if
the litmus of twilight could easily go
either way

The heart too
ready for any such
                    tug

The Meadow

I follow the path through the meadow
stream on one side
willows, fireweed on the other.

Last winter we skied here
your stride long, loping
the legato swish of your skis
your poles planted briefly in snow
one
and then another
like the years of a marriage.

Where the track disappeared
you broke trail over wind-crusted snow
indenting whiteness with
parallel lines for me to follow,
gliding.

But today water flows freely
pours like glass over sandbars
whispers against the banks —
an intake of breath
                    and its release
the long conversation of water and meadow.

Ahead, the valley
turns north between black arms of spruce
toward the headwaters.

Is this what it comes to:
a narrow valley vanishing?
Or is the true source downstream,
at the confluence, where fish
pour into the curve of
water's abundance,
their momentary shadows
sliding through silver?

Inland

Elsewhere, the tide moves
to a different heartbeat,
not the long diastole
of the interior,
ice lingering in April on the riverbank,
cottonwoods reluctant to concede
a change of season, their fragrance
leaked, little by little
into the arteries of spring.

The sea teaches a less cautious rhythm,
the ebb and flow
of four fifths of the planet
empties and fills and
empties the wide bay
the shoreline we walked in summer,
tang of iodine in the air,
our hands not touching
because there seemed no need,
the waves beside us an endless
pulse at the wrist of the world.

Does this explain why you
have forgotten me,
because I live inland,
because the tides here move so slowly
you mistake them
for the passage of years,
because you believe
there is no salt in the air?

I thought of you again today,
in a field at the edge of melting snow
where last summer's grass lay flat, its stems
curved like ripples in sand —
blue sky above
    ready to beat.

Penelope

You tell me you dream of knitting.
Through the long dark your fingers loop
invisible threads, needles click like
cooling metal, like the letters
of an antique telegraphy.
You are making a sweater for a ghost,
you tell me,
the nights are that cold.

But by day you unravel it all,
keep a husband happy
in your comfortable kitchen,
watch his butter knife busy
over slices of toast.

What is left of constancy?
Where is the bow
that none can bend, the horn that
keeps its music to itself? Your closets
are full of the customary evasions:
overcoats, spare light bulbs for the hall,
shoes.

Only the ancient dog sprawls
all day in the sun, wanders
oceans of sleep and dreams the relentless
simplicities of love.

When you approach,
his breath quickens,
                   paws
twitch.

Vernal Equinox

When you say *bread*
do you mean what's held between
thumb and fingers
like pliant halves of a pure idea
    a longing you could break
along crisp partitions of an abstract hunger;
or do you mean
        gluten
        a taste of salt
        the weight of a loaf in your arms:
its dark crust, its white flesh

When you say *love* do you mean
the open lotus of the left hand
after your fingers have launched the heart into air
into the arc and
        twang of the racket — a green ball
served across a net into
whatever volley may follow;
        or do you mean
a clench of muscle near the diaphragm at that uneasy
point of balance between breath and digestion
inner and outer   something unarguable
that tells you the game's up
tells you
this is the moment
you stand to lose everything

the moment the seasons change,
        break
their old rhythms of departure and approach,
and exhale, like yeast, a new passion for the sun:

that same intoxication,
leap over the net
    that doomed *beau geste*

Red Truck

This morning a bear dead by the side of the road.

In the evening three deer caught
in the corner of an eye among branches on the twilit passage home.
Always this coming and going — the iterations,
we want to believe, of an innocent life. But do we

choose avoidance? Is there a moment when we say: I want
the hum of tires on dry pavement to continue,
Les Violons du Roy on Radio 2 to elaborate the
counterpoint of Bach to its end, everything to pass unscathed, no
amble of fur from ditch, no blunt impact of blood
and guts wedged in the wheel well, steering lost, the mess
of culpability?

Or is it luck
        what becomes true and what not? The choices we
think we make and how they play themselves out — a red truck
driven on asphalt at so many miles per hour, odometer measuring
the pulse of whatever is possible while

somewhere in the scrub a heart contracts

something wild that knows neither truth nor lies but only
a fading of light, currents of air, the impulsive
firing of a synapse, launches itself across the road

headlong into a journey
just as random
a margin of error just as wide
        as that?

And then

*That's that
the days say,
and click shut.*

Or so you tell yourself, as if
forgetting were as simple as turning
the little window card on its string,
pulling down blinds.
As if words were a ledger and not
a displacement, a world
permanently altered.
        As if
elk had never looked out from
the edge of trees
where the road (do you remember) curves
to the right
10:00 pm
a Thursday   the night moonless,
their breathing slow, particular —
like someone's foot in a door
insisting.

We can't will what we know away,
unspeak daylight like
books we might fiddle
to balance
uneasy limits of the accountable.

Nothing is as we once thought
we knew it — what is true, what
is not, these
fragments in our hands we can't put down.
Or go home.
Or say: *The words, yes, but not
their meaning.*

Who knows what elk dream
drifting in the dark, what
business they think they're about? Not what is shut
but what remains open —
                    a taste on the tongue
for the thing
we have not yet thought
to say.

There is a sadness

when we know we are safe,
when wheels touch ground
and all that's left
is addresses, waves, taxis home,

nothing with an edge,
an unsettling flex of wings,
our fingertips
nervous on the armrest,

the things we could not say because
of the noise of engines, how we banked
among clouds till we lost all sense
of the earth, memory of anything

but plunging glances
sideways at blue, the world
all vertigo, not even a nod
toward vanished horizons.

The sadness is
there was too much air, too much
room to manoeuvre, and we not
desperate enough to

cut through the unimaginable
vortex of lightning, plunge into
the dark heart of the thunderhead
as if these were the last

moments of the world and we
about to burst from the anvil
            ringing
            tempered
a million miles from anywhere.

Noir

On nights like this your mind stumbles
through the streambed of sleep,
knocks against stones.
Whatever flight has brought you
to this fording is not escape
but only you
flailing against the current.

Or other nightmares of flight:
hydro lines above the road,
treetops you cannot clear
however much you haul back
on the Cessna's yoke.

The interminable runway of such nights.

You tell yourself these fugitive dreams
are just scenes remembered
from old movies, celluloid
spilling through sprockets, the flicker
between light and dark
merely the eye's illusion of pursuit.

But you know you know
better, know you will wake
with bruised ankles and sore arms,
the machinery of everything you can't ignore
still roaring in your ears, and you
still driven, still earthbound
as the final reel turns and turns, its clatter
the clack of stone against stone,

the recurrent nightmare
of each dawn,
                    the beating
        of your heart.

Arrow Lake

If the wind blew,
tossed brown arms of grass among these rocks, if waves
however landlocked, however gentle
broke at the foot of cliffs,
if smoke from forest fires drifted
across the
    blue of the sky, if
the ferry beyond the bay seemed less
unmoving,   the pulse of its engines
less like   if the mirror of the lake
weren't as clear as
if the mountains did not remind me of
        if the sun
if you

But
    the grasses
are caught in their fissures of rock:
brown blade, golden
seed head,
rock, lake, sky, this
clement world where the *Galena Bay* floats
above its image
        on a lake that was once a river —
glacier above the far shore
a faint smudge on water

as if
    a brush had
wiped something from slate

Poste Restante

He can no longer remember who died
at the Schönbrunn in the same bed where
someone else had been born,
no longer recall more than the passing
warmth of October sun on ochre,
the creak of leather from the saddles
of the Royal Lippizaners, a rococo vault,
the sound of hooves on sawdust,
the fine rhythm of their sinewy reach
toward elegance — a museum piece,
like the packet of letters she tells him years later
she has kept and reads on winter afternoons
as an exercise of memory,
                    knowing nothing
of the tree-lined street whose name,
if truth were told, he has forgotten,
where he climbed the stone steps
of the *Postamtbüro* to receive and send
ordinary news of the weather,
of the changing season, the states of the heart —
an unremarkable correspondence
which the clerk behind the wicket
nevertheless would not deliver till she verified
he was who he was, would not send
till she stamped each envelope
with proof of just how far they were
from anywhere either of them
would ever recognize.

In the trees

light fades among leaves
like a kind of amnesia,
the backward brush of a hand
after erasure.

Memory, that kind of palimpsest.

(What did we ever have
to say to each other, anyway?)

Small birds curl their feet
around branches.
There may be nests —
strands of hair, bits of twig,
a fragment of blue eggshell
frail as
            the timbre of your voice.

The names we failed to learn
for birds.

Liebeslied

The soprano wears a wine-coloured gown,
  the radio says,
the colour of pinot noir.

I am driving home in March twilight.
Bare trees slip by,
snow is diminishing in the ditches.

Three time zones away a voice in Toronto
translates the German text
of Schumann's Spanish love songs
  (Robert Schumann, not Clara.
  Before he went mad,
  before she met Brahms).

In the depths of my heart, the soprano sings,
  her gown (which she is no longer wearing,
        the concert having ended,
        of course, weeks ago)
  shimmering like heartbreak,
In the depths of my soul, I suffer.

A pickup truck passes.

I wonder what the verb was in Spanish,
what journeys of translation might lead
back from this sky
  (the colour of nothing in particular)
to the southern vineyard where it all began,
a melody dreamt at the start
somewhere in the grey streets of Leipzig.

I watch a coyote lope across the road
his paws precise as fingers on a scale.
But it's too early for serenades
    (too much light, too much human traffic
    coming and going)
and he disappears into a grove of aspen
without a backward glance,
never once
    breaking his stride.

Beach Glass

At the edge of the hayfield
there is nothing left to say.

Stubble
like the tide at ebb
lingers at a line of clover the machinery
could not reach, or ignored
as superfluous,

blossoms of pink and white
like beach glass
ground in the wind.

The story here is only a remnant,
an edge
you might follow for miles and
get no closer to anything —
not the tangle of grass, after-image
        of the sea, or pale headland
of trees.

                All afternoon
the fenceline of that loss.
Those waves.

THREE

The Reservoir

Years ago you sent me a poem in which
stars fell flaming into the Canmore reservoir
etching the sky above the mountains with their light.
It was your last letter. It was winter.

Today I am hiking with others
up a gulch where the Kootenai traveled
a thousand years ago, and where climbers
now dangle from the rockface
spread-eagled like pictographs.

The trail we climb feels like
a ritual journey, gravel pouring
around ankles, filling our eyes
with dust, saying to the heart:
your goal
eludes you, you're
            not there yet,
the path ahead
still at least
a
thousand years.

But we gain the top:
a lake,
an arc of dam,
a metal guardrail.
Wind blows from the west.
Water laps the edge of a road that,
had we known, could have
brought us here in no time.
There is a chain-link fence.

What else?

Did I expect to see your stars
glowing in the depths?
Streaks of submarine light
like the fuel rods of a dying reactor?
The landscape radioactive? Holograms on rocks?

Nothing lasts a thousand years.
Tourists erode ochre, climbers rappel down.
Even stars have a half-life
as brief
as that of words.

I turn to the vista
to where Canmore sprawls
and see that I have been mistaken.
A second body of water is
perched above the valley floor,
its shore a circle of white as distinct, as obvious
as if a finger were tracing it on stone.

It is the reservoir. It is in sunlight.
Wind scuffs its surface.
Starless. Blue.

La reproduction interdite

It is our backs that reveal the most, you said
à propos of something we must have talked about
before you turned to strike a match,
your shoulders hunched against the wind, hands cupped
the way they might have been
had you been bringing me a firefly from the garden
    (had there been a garden).
But whatever ignited there, all I saw was
a wisp of smoke vanishing downwind
like a term subtracted from
an imbalanced equation: a moment
greater than or equal to, or
a moment less than
anything we might have said instead.

Unless your leaving wasn't like algebra at all
but like Magritte's mirror
refusing the solace of reflection,
something we could at least face — if only
the thin comfort of an infinite regression: days
coming at us down the wind bearing
                        grit
                        tumbleweeds
                        an end of winter
however diminished abrasive devoid of hope I don't care, but not
this silent turning away, the cold
theorems of departure,
        not even a glance over your shoulder,
or farewell
or offer of a final, lit
                cigarette.

El Niño

Or we could talk about the weather,
borrow a book from the library, catch the evening news
and look at satellite photos of yet another
frontal system skirting the Gulf of Alaska,
swirls of cloud as indistinct as the blurred
evasions that circulate in the public domain
and call themselves a life,
call themselves winter.

It is snowfall we need,
wind cutting through us breathless
from an Arctic High, the authentic voice
of a season that insists
on absolute possession: a clarity
whose only accurate measure
                          is margin of risk,

a language the white
emptiness of the land makes us own —
makes us own up to.

The trees say:

Look, this is for you,
these napkins of cloud,
a tableland
spread among fields,
starched hills unfolded, blue
sky over shimmering
canopy of leaves where sunrise
offers the hors d'oeuvre of day
on a monogrammed plate:
This is home.
(The table d'hote,
a gilt fork,
a spoon.)

*

But yours is a wilder hunger, the
gaping vertiginous space where
animals gnaw on cliffs, the flanks
of mountains, where ravens
fling themselves into the raucous
throat of wind, the jagged, the in-
decorous skyline a serrated knife
hot in your hand.

*

At dusk deer at the edge of a field
watch you, want
nothing: trees, a filter of
light, flick
            of ear, grass underfoot
and
      then what?
Live
from hand to mouth, believe there is
sustenance in this
surely
somewhere?

Lente, lente

Days before snow
the bowl of autumn overflows
with the souls of the lost,
the spent currency of trees
with which the season thinks to purchase
an architecture of stars,
a wash of rain,
promises of the empyrean delivered
to the tips of fingers.

Of course you know better.

But would you unwrite the bargain
of this residual hope,
these lingering constellations,
empty the bowl
the way you have drained the garden tap?

Winter is everywhere.
Heaven loves us not.
Horses gallop at midnight
through the Pine Pass
while in the bare arms of trees
the northern lights perform their seductive dance.

Let the chafer of their fire
warm the blood. Dip the heart
one last time
in that green.

Write your name above the trees.

Laundry Day

a poem ending with a line from Richard Wilbur

Surely this bruise of a planet, this haemorrhage,
these pixels of the eternal Vietnam of the world,
this landscape all blot, all varicose-veined,
stained, this ember, this blood-dimmed tide,
damned spot
must ebb, must out.

Surely the knotted lanyard of history will
hoist a white flag, whatever ragged
T-shirt it can.

And we dream of cupcakes, of penguins,
the innocence of sheets,
reload the bombers with nuns,
send them wimpling over the suburbs to fall
like black-and-white blessings, their
beads clinking benediction,
rain.

Let us see the end of crimson. Let it be loosed.
Let there be no tatters, no
wringing of hands, no reasons,
no knives in rut.

Let there be nothing on earth but laundry.

Crowbar

Is this all that remains
of your tools,
of a lifetime's accumulation of the useful
and suitable,
of the whole abundant chest of
the finely honed, the apt extensions
of a restless brain:
               this claw, this
black stump,
raw metal stick, this
one implement of pure destruction
whose dream
is the shrieking of nails?

Why not
an adze, a saw, a set of chisels with
splayed wooden handles —
tools of benign intent,
that cut with the ordered habits of an analytic mind?
Why this refuser of argument,
this mere lever,
wielder of pepper-spray,
this interrogator of the superfluous,
steel question mark that fits
so unwillingly, so

perfectly
in my hand.

Anything but the Moon

Plenty left even so —
bushes, trees
rows of cabbage in the garden
a horse shifting its weight
beside the fence,
shapes of this and that
in the easeful dark.

No moonrise,
no ivory baton raised
to signal an intake of breath,
no downbeat,
flood of silver quavers
spilling over the world,
silk shimmering
on the dance-floor, bodies
luminous with reflected light.

None of that,
the old tune's played out
grooves worn
clean off the shellac —
too many dizzy lovers
spinning round the spindle,
too much heartfelt
scratching at the sky.

Learn to live in the earth's eclipse,
the long conical shadow
of the way things are.
No visible scar
but the heart's faint tug,
blurred memory of ebb and flow
occluding the fixed stars.

What could you want otherwise —
the ocean
its tides
handle of the gramophone wound up again,
that old four-four rhythm waxing and
waning in the blood, something round
above the hills to howl at?

Nothing but ghosts in the air,
the mist words leave on a mirror,
old lies retold —
of Diana and her bow,
of Icarus rising from the sea,
of his urge to temp the sky again
to soar above the plowman
                              and turn
without wings   toward the music,

embrace
the open arms of a pale
new moon.

Mute

Try to remember other nights,
starlit, with
dew and grass underfoot,
billows of cloud across the sky
like full sleeves of the day's drama
repeated in mime,
all shape and gesture
without heat.

Or else the moon in whiteface
stooping to the earth,
one arm flung back, the other
bending to pluck something unseen
with an excessive delicacy
that makes a stem seem
stubbornly to resist
the stylized moment of its severance.

There was a time you could
believe in the body as easily as that,
its exaggerated simplicity,
the unspoken eloquence of
everything it touched freed
from any further need
to be named.

But you have forgotten that,
know only the black and grey
of a landscape extinguished years ago
when tail-lights crested the hill and left you
scriptless
to the reticence of night,
left you thinking
you could not possibly go on.

Left you going on.

En vacances

Today it is June. Everywhere
sunlight filters through new leaves of aspen.
Beyond the trees, fields are flushed
with a green as pale and startled
as tourists in a piazza, awkward
in their shorts.

You saved all winter for this,
but perhaps you expected something else,
something more than sun and colour,
a change of clothes, wanted more
from photosynthesis than a predictable
summer romance, a mere
extravagance of dapple and breeze.
You thought these moments of unfurling
would be a different country,
a place where the light would fall
just so — on water
                    through branches, on the line of
a shoulder or arm, the movement of hands
parting ferns.

But summer is summer
and you must face the facts.
These hours of daylight are merely botany
on tour: germination,
                a few afternoons on the beach,
                bus tour to the ruins,
                        abscission.
While you breathe the scent of cottonwood
the trees think only of notching up
another ring in the old heartwood;
birds in the canopy twitter
little folk-songs;
hayfields hawk their souvenirs.

You have just arrived
and already you long for home.

Reading the Aftermath

Plows are out clearing the arteries.

Clouds slip by above the city, pour
over the hills,
the blue finger of the west traces
a story too new
    too difficult
to trust to the eye alone.
You need to feel the words
to get the drift,
                 to understand
love's possible after all.

Though it's not what you'd think,
not a matter of the heart,
all its blunt syllabic scraping
the way it pumps out meaning
    (the way it falters),
but of something lifted,
               an ease of breath,
the brief clemency
of whatever you can say that's true:

The air that fills your lungs.
The sky.

FOUR

I'll let you in ...

but there are no secrets to this art,
   no cunning entrance
   or galleries of stalagmite and
   stalactite, claustrophobic squeezing
   through fissures of limestone, a balance
   between what is deposited
   and what dissolved, no *son et lumière*
   of the dark, the ghostly organ pipes
   of a world turned in on itself,
   hearts collapsing
   like black holes
   when the headlamps turn off,

or if there are
they are harder than that:
   the way granite refuses water,
   offers no way in,
   how the foot is lead and the eye spills
   downstream over heather
   to a cottage where fullers
   beat wet cloth against stone,
   filling the gaps between warp
   and weft
      water and rock,

the songs they sing.

This is not a sermon, this is a landscape

Beauty is neither
the beginning nor the end. The arms of these hills
opening to the north west
gather squalls,
                      mottle the lake with
light, with flurries,   or else bend
inward round this beach, fold ice into a bay
where winter still binds water,
                      waveless, to land.

The steeple of Our Lady of Good Hope
(thin, lovely)
looks out over a plain of white,
a history of wind
             which today skims ice bare, teaching
there is neither innocence nor guilt in this world,
that everything
is both relic and dream.

Here the seasons move forward and back, gain hope
and lose it, the way
at night, asleep in your cabin by the shore
you either hear   or don't
the lake-ice shift,
which it does   and does
regardless.

One day the church will burn
but you'll remember where it stood
(antique, impossible)
a landmark
    a point of view
      the place you start,

what you cherish as the world ends,
or as it begins.

Nocturne

Cochrane, Alberta

What he remembers is dark foothills
rolling beneath the sky, a few stars
    crickets —
whatever imagination can invent to
summon a summer night:
footsteps on gravel,
a faint luminescence of dust,
                absence of wind

Some things become true in daylight:
the small town on a map, its name,
its silent streets,
white clapboard on the Esso station,
the journey back to the car they had left behind,
empty of gas,
dust billowing in the box of a pickup, the morning sun

already hot on the land

But what persists is what may not be true:
the sound of her voice,
        their breathing,
what each one said,
how they fell into step,
the gas flares in the distance (their flames
    burning off everything
    unnecessary)

So that in the end what remains is night,
a gas can in his hand to bring back
all he thought they'd need

the purpose of the journey

the wherewithal to go on

Water/Ice

The glacier delivers him up
in the end
to the light

not bone by bone
as fragments
shreds of cloth buried in silt
an empty quiver
its flint-tipped arrows
spilt

but whole
the way a diver,
returning, breaks through
the refractive surface
of water
into air

limbs released from the long
embrace of ice, skin
once again the crisp
particular edge of sense,
a hand
ready for the bow

He has lost nothing
in the long liquid arc,
the blue silence
of memory inching its way
across bedrock,
save breath
and a certain innocence of time

For breath there is wind
thrumming over the ribcage,
for innocence
the slow certainty of the world,
the wrinkled surface of things,
of ice on its precarious
journey, seracs
leaning like flints,
throwing sparks into the tinder
of mountain light

what eludes you

like a fish
like clouds

the surface of things
or their underside
reflects, ripples
a trick of light

you move from
element to element
    a lungful of air
    the cold slip
    of water from skin
always leaving

always you
or the world drawing a line:
here is what is
here is all
you can't have

but still
the trout,
still the hiss of rain
    the lines of its fall

a lake
        the world
breathing it in

Juniper

Halfway to the skyline what
chance of finding the right stone —
palm-sized, cupped —
just right for a heart
halfway
          to overflowing

These tipped strata yield only
what scree the seasons peel off
whatever shuffles, shears, whatever sun
makes empty, memory
choking among stones

The mountain is nothing but a history of dust,
a wave that cannot break
till it prove
the point of its indifference
to the wind, the sky

Still,
I return with these few berries.
                              They,
not time, will wear rock down —
whatever is gathered in the hands,
a world, a few words,
anything simple:
     like rain
     like forest
          like this pungent, spherical, ever-spiny
blue

Hollyhocks

Alcea rosea, var. Officinalis Alba:
    pure white,
    the five-petalled flowers
    your mind thinks of first,
    as clean as the slice and flash of skates
    on ice, chaste as the knitted toques of girls,
    the buds of mittens where
    stamens of fingers cluster —
    leaves glabrous and heart-shaped,
    finely toothed.

Alcea rosea, var. Chater's Double Apricot,
    Peaches 'N' Cream, Powder Puff Mixed,
    and many more, all the colours
    you were promised would never fade, double blooms
    in cream and pink and citron tulle
    like rosettes on the fins of the baby-blue Buick
    the day you were caught in the
    pop of flashbulbs, the swirl of confetti bright
    as whitewalls scrubbed with steelwool,
    fistfuls of it clutched in someone's hand.

Alcea rosea, var. Nigra:
    the impossible black flower
    which your friends insist is merely
    purple, or inky-brown, or at most
    a dark dark shade of maroon
    but which you know is more dangerous than that:
    as irrefutable as the herbaceous borders of dreams
    on nights when the moon has set
    and when light attains the perfect
    absence of colour —
    flowers as dense, as black,
    as possible as that.

Alcea pallida and *Alcea setosa*:
    the precursors of garden varieties:
    pink and white, native to
    E. Europe and to Cyprus, Turkey and Crete,
    simple petals, stems to 2m
    growing in fallow fields and rocky places,
    requiring little but heat and sun, dry soil
    and an open aspect —
    a chosen neglect needing nothing
    but the habit of inadvertence.

The Path Back

1

I dropped a stone into the pitcher
of the raven's beak,
and then another,

but he refused to sing,
let alone speak.

This was when the mountains were dark.
Now they are darker still.

Ravens are like that;
even more so stones.

2

The spring on Tunnel Mountain
flows only after dark.

The moon with its canteen.

How far would you walk to see this?

3

We come to the mountains
as to a mirror,
                    fearing light.

God too was timid,
till deer opened their eyes,
the summits
turned their faces.

4

I can only tell you that
beauty follows the valley.

I can only tell you.

The river is both open
and icebound. The path
always returning.

Divide

He hikes the cordillera following water:
streams, waterfalls,
the relentless energy of descent,
hearing the mainspring of gravity unwind,
a metronome of droplets gathering all that
spray, that clattering brilliant
wetness in,
mountainsides of sprung rhythm
cascading toward cadence — the little
lakes where it all collects,
moose wading at the shoreline,
held chord of a loon reflecting itself
in the fermata of twilight.

Yet his eye moves against the current
seeking streams that diminish
upward, following the edge of water
as it curves from stone to stone to
the progressive simplicity of the alpine:
trees left behind, juniper
little bursts of saxifrage among the rocks
and then just rocks,
the clean geometric wind of cirques and summits
where flowing water is gradually
reduced to the pure idea of
single drops melting
from snow,
a marmot whistling in the cold air.

Do all needs originate in snow,
its surface cupped by summer sunlight
cool spray against knees
as he kicks footsteps
upward toward a col between two peaks
and to a skyline which divides   what —
air from rock
sound from silence, or simply
one watershed from another?

What is the glacier on the other side
but another tempo of water,
a long bowstroke
drawn across his field of vision —
ice falls, delicate lines of moraine,
all the stately sadness
of the heart at its source?
A river
beginning to flow north
toward the Arctic Ocean.

The Jewellers

She leans on the glass cabinet
as over a parapet,
face dazzled by the updraft of light, the eye's
slow drift above a crystal diorama,
each diamond a serac,
a tweezer of phosphorus
blinding itself in the brilliance of arctic air.

No blood on these diamonds,
just a pure white genesis,
the certificate of origin she seeks,
believing the weight of the right words
can equal permanence

as in the final open page of Scott's diary
in its cabinet in London:
It seems a pity, he wrote,
his companions dead on either side,
but I do not think I can write more

as the cold of that disastrous journey
compressed itself
into a pure white light,
into the eloquence of finality
that links obsession with history.
The hard edge. The fatal
clarity of ice.

Lost Wax, Midwinter

Not light
burnished on the rim of the new moon,
the sharp-edged metallurgy of stars,
but its absence, hours of darkness
molten into the negative space of the heart
where what is not displaces
what never was, if truth were told,
more than etched idea —

cycles of a moon
we once saw through glass,
our leavetaking held tenderly in its arms,
the orbits of the world as
ductile then as silver, as quick to hope,
not honed like this
to hardness

cold against skin

Years before this solstice
you wrote something
about *the constellations of desire*,
although I can't remember what or when,
only that the dark was
figured then, filigreed, the sky peopled
with gods and beasts, their gestures
a pattern against the cold
against night   this aftermath
this final pouring out

this pouring in

Phytolith

A blue Plymouth
abandoned among willows
has you believing you have discovered something,
a residual clue, the shape of a former habitation
or the gesture your arms might assume
years later, when you have forgotten a woman you danced with
even her name
although your body still retains relics of that music
(your hand on her waist) the few brief measures
when neither you nor she
either led or followed, but lived a movement
as effortless and commonplace as a key thrust into a pocket,
as walking away from a car never
doubting your return — the click
of cooling metal behind you
no more final
than the flit of tanagers from a branch.

If you had known anything about anything then —
the way departure deposits itself like silica
in the moments you believe yourself
most undeniably alive — if you had had an inkling,
you might have turned
to catch the light glinting off chrome, might have
thought of something fitting to say:
>   *Goodbye*, perhaps, or
>   *I will remember you always.*

Perseids

To slip under the surface of the night
like a gloved hand inserted in luggage —
a formality
which never stops at merely that:
    what belongs to you
    what you have left unattended,
those blunt questions of intent

all night long
a border you cannot cross, like the sheet of glass
beyond which the neighbour's dog
refuses disclosure,
sticks to his story about
what matters and what does not, repeating it
over and over for anyone
who might want to hear

Beyond his back meteors slice the dark,
flick their
sleight of hand like messages
smuggled through barbed wire
or a package flung
from a window, a lie, streak of light, brief
truth which
may have nothing to do with you
but which is now yours, a thing
wrapped in tinfoil which you
can't explain:
        bright
        incriminating —
                the sky
a suitcase of contraband

This Grey Light

It is to the dead we turn
in the end
for the lessons of love.

A thin drizzle among trees
in a light
that could be dawn, could be
        any time
as far as this hillside is concerned,
daylight being not
what measures time here,
    nor the spill of lupins
    nor the silent
coming and going of snow,

nor yet these brief visits from
the living who wander
among spruce, among these graves,
    our solemn need
to find the names of sorrow,
    our bewilderment
that it all comes to this,
        everything we love.

Only the spruce themselves
are calibrated to loss,
to the imperceptible way roots
absorb rain and soil,
                alter
bones into concentric rings,
turn time into timber as if
the heart weren't meant for more
        than this.

But it is.

There is a morning of rain
much heavier than today,
the soil still mounded fresh,
the narrow blade of a shovel
inserted at the crest of earth
        a few inches,
as much as grief can allow itself,
        as much as
the seedling's roots need
to settle   to get a grip
to get the feel of
the dark damp texture of all that will
not now befall.

Lupin, monkshood, a bush of
mountain huckleberry
        drip in the rain.
Among them
a little burst of needles glistens
green in the grey light.

Mallory

1

He lies on a mountainside of stones,
a pearl-fisher lost
in his dive for the summit,
arms in mid-stroke reaching uphill
through strands of rope
like kelp, like sea wrack,
                              a tangle
in the tides of wind.
He is an ivory yardstick
counting distance not in rope-lengths,
height not with the wheezing
altimeter of the lungs,
but with this simple measure of bone:
an arm
a leg
a posture of longing.

2

Somewhere among stones the camera
remains lost, a fist clenching its
handful of secrets,
frozen emulsion
the blurred memory of wind, footprints
ascending across snow
                     or stopped,
the end of the journey
a final moment
forever
inconclusive.

3

It is not a rock
Sisyphus rolls up the mountain
but the burden
of open space   breath
a movement
not of air but of the emptiness
between molecules, the indigo
blankness of sky —
not the false perspective of the eye
where rock stops, but
the final edge
                    the end, at last, to it all.
Nothing
        but the wind of the planet
and the heart
gulping it in.

Acknowledgements

My profound thanks to:

Jean McKay, who has been the aesthetic and moral conscience
of these poems from the beginning.

Sue Sinclair for her fierce intelligence and impeccable editorial eye.

Jan Zwicky and Don McKay for their unbounded generosity
and encouragement.

Donna Kane for her friendship and pragmatic honesty
along the way.

Many other writers and friends who have nourished this work.
Among them: Patrick Friesen, Maureen Scott Harris, Jan Horner,
Ken Howe, Isabel Huggan, Ross Leckie, Dennis Lee, Lorri Neilsen
Glenn, Jay Ruzesky, Rhea Tregebov, Jill Wigmore.

Some of these poems have previously appeared in *The Malahat
Review*, *The Fiddlehead*, *Grain*, *Pottersfield Portfolio* and *Event*. I am
grateful to the editors of these magazines, especially to Marlene
Cookshaw and Liz Phillips.

Thanks also to the Banff Centre for a very productive residency
during the 2001 Writing Studio.

Above all, thanks to Bridget, Emilie and Ros for sustaining me with
their love and tolerance.